THE NEGROES AT PORT ROYAL.

REPORT

OF

E. L. PIERCE, GOVERNMENT AGENT,

TO THE

HON. SALMON P. CHASE,

SECRETARY OF THE TREASURY.

BOSTON:
PUBLISHED BY R. F. WALLCUT,
No. 221 WASHINGTON STREET.
1862.

REPORT.

PORT ROYAL, February 3, 1862.

TO THE HON. SALMON P. CHASE,

Secretary of the Treasury:

DEAR SIR,—My first communication to you was mailed on the third day after my arrival. The same day, I mailed two letters to benevolent persons in Boston, mentioned in my previous communications to you, asking for contributions of clothing, and for a teacher or missionary to be sent, to be supported by the charity of those interested in the movement, to both of which favorable answers have been received. The same day, I commenced a tour of the largest islands, and ever since have been diligently engaged in anxious examinations of the modes of culture—the amount and proportions of the products—the labor required for them—the life and disposition of the laborers upon them—their estimated numbers—the treatment they have received from their former masters, both as to the labor required of them, the provisions and clothing allowed to them, and the discipline imposed—their habits, capacities, and desires, with special reference to their being fitted for useful citizenship—and generally whatever concerned the well-being, present and future, of the territory and its people. Visits have also been made to the communities collected at Hilton Head and Beaufort, and conferences held with the authorities, both naval and military, and other benevolent persons interested in the welfare of these people, and the wise and speedy reörganization of society here. No one can be impressed more than myself with the uncertainty of conclusions drawn from experiences and reflections gathered in so brief a period, however industriously and wisely occupied. Nevertheless, they may be of some service to those who have not been privileged with an equal opportunity.

Of the plantations visited, full notes have been taken of seventeen, with reference to number of negroes in all; of field hands; amount of cotton and corn raised, and how much per acre; time and mode of producing and distributing manure; listing, planting, cultivating, picking and ginning cotton; labor required of each hand; allowance of food and clothing; the capacities of the laborers; their wishes and feelings, both as to themselves and their masters. Many of the above points could be determined by other sources, such as persons at the North familiar with the region, and publications. The inquiries were, however, made with the double purpose of acquiring the information and testing the capacity of the persons inquired of. Some of the leading results of the examination will now be submitted.

An estimate of the number of plantations open to cultivation, and of the persons upon the territory protected by the forces of the United States, if only approximate to the truth, may prove convenient in providing a proper system of administration. The following islands are thus protected, and the estimated number of plantations upon each is given:—

Port Royal, ...	65	St. Helena, ...	50
Ladies', ...	30	Hilton Head, ...	16
Parry, including Horse, .	6	Pinckney, ...	5
Cat, ...	1	Bull, including Barratria,	2
Cane, ...	1	Daufuskie, . . .	5
Dathaw, ...	4	Hutchinson and Fenwick,	6
Coosaw, ...	2		
Morgan, ...	2		195

Or about two hundred in all.

There are several other islands thus protected, without plantations, as Otter, Pritchard, Fripp, Hunting and Phillips. Lemon and Daw have not been explored by the agents engaged in collecting cotton.

The populous island of North Edisto, lying in the direction of Charleston, and giving the name to the finest cotton, is still visited by the rebels. A part near Botany Bay Island is commanded by the guns of one of our war vessels, under which a colony of one thousand negroes sought protection, where they have been temporarily subsisted from its stores. The number has within a few days been stated to have increased to 2300. Among these, great destitution is said to prevail. Even to this number, as the negroes acquire confidence in us, large additions are likely every week to be made. The whole island can be safely farmed as soon as troops can be spared for the purpose of occupation. But not counting the plantations of this island, the number on Port Royal, Ladies', St. Helena, Hilton Head, and the smaller islands, may be estimated at 200 plantations.

In visiting the plantations, I endeavored to ascertain with substantial accuracy the number of persons upon them, without, however, expecting to determine the precise number. On that of Thomas Aston Coffin, at Coffin Point, St. Helena, there were 260, the largest found on any one visited. There were 130 on that of Dr. J. W. Jenkins, 120 on that of the Eustis estate, and the others range from 80 to 38, making an average of 81 to a plantation. These, however, may be ranked among the best peopled plantations, and forty to each may be considered a fair average. From these estimates, a population of 8000 negroes on the islands, now safely protected by our forces, results.

Of the 600 at the camp at Hilton Head, about one-half should be counted with the aforesaid plantations whence they have come. Of the 600 at Beaufort, one-third should also be reckoned with the plantations. The other fraction in each case should be added to the 8000 in computing the population now thrown on our protection.

The negroes on Ladies' and St. Helena Islands have quite generally remained on their respective plantations, or if absent, but temporarily, visiting wives or relatives. The dispersion on Port Royal and Hilton Head Islands has been far greater, the people of the former going to Beaufort in considerable numbers, and of the latter to the camp at Hilton Head.

Counting the negroes who have gone to Hilton Head and Beaufort from places now protected by our forces as still attached to the plantations, and to that extent not swelling the 8000 on plantations, but adding thereto the usual negro population of Beaufort, as also the negroes who have fled to Beaufort and Hilton Head from places not yet occupied by our forces, and adding also the colony at North Edisto, and we must now have thrown upon our hands, for whose present and future we must provide, from 10,000 to 12,000 persons—probably nearer the latter than the former number. This number is rapidly increasing. This week, forty-eight escaped from a single plantation near Grahamville, on the main land, held by the rebels, led by the driver, and after four days of trial and peril, hidden by day and threading the waters with their boats by night, evading the rebel pickets, joyfully entered our camp at Hilton Head. The accessions at Edisto are in larger number, and according to the most reasonable estimates, it would only require small advances by our troops, not involving a general engagement or even loss of life, to double the number which would be brought within our lines.

A fact derived from the Census of 1860 may serve to illustrate the responsibility now devolving on the Government. This County of Beaufort had a population of slaves in proportion of $82\frac{8}{10}$ of the whole,—a proportion only exceeded by seven other counties in the United States, viz.: one in South Carolina, that of Georgetown; three in Mississippi, those of Bolivar, Washington and Issequena; and three in Louisiana, those of Madison, Tensas and Concordia.

An impression prevails that the negroes here have been less cared for than in most other rebel districts. If this be so, and a beneficent reform shall be achieved here, the experiment may anywhere else be hopefully attempted.

The former white population, so far as can be ascertained, are rebels, with one or two exceptions. In January, 1861, a meeting of the planters on St. Helena Island was held, of which Thomas Aston Coffin was chairman. A vote was passed, stating its exposed condition, and offering their slaves to the Governor of South Carolina, to aid in building earth mounds, and calling on him for guns to place upon them. A copy of the vote, probably in his own handwriting, and signed by Mr. Coffin, was found in his house.

It is worthy of note that the negroes now within our lines are there by the invitation of no one; but they were on the soil when our army began its occupation, and could not have been excluded, except by violent transportation. A small proportion have come in from the main land, evading the pickets of the enemy and our own,—something easily done in an extensive country, with whose woods and creeks they are familiar.

The only exportable crop of this region is the long staple Sea Island cotton, raised with more difficulty than the coarser kind, and bringing a higher price. The agents of the Treasury Department expect to gather some 2,500,000 pounds of ginned cotton the present year, nearly all of which had been picked and stored before the arrival of our forces. Considerable quantities have not been picked at all, but the crop for this season was unusually good. Potatoes and corn are raised only for consumption on the plantations,—corn being raised at the rate of only twenty-five bushels per acre.

Such features in plantation life as will throw light on the social questions now anxiously weighed deserve notice.

In this region, the master, if a man of wealth, is more likely to have his main residence at Beaufort, sometimes having none on the plantation, but having one for the driver, who is always a negro. He may, however, have one, and an expensive one, too, as in the case of Dr. Jenkins, at St. Helena, and yet pass most of his time at Beaufort, or at the North. The plantation in such cases is left almost wholly under the charge of an overseer. In some cases, there is not even a house for an overseer, the plantation being superintended by the driver, and being visited by the overseer living on another plantation belonging to the same owner. The houses for the overseers are of an undesirable character. Orchards of orange or fig trees are usually planted near them.

The field hands are generally quartered at some distance—eighty or one hundred rods—from the overseer's or master's house, and are ranged in a row, sometimes in two rows, fronting each other. They are sixteen feet by twelve, each appropriated to a family, and in some cases divided with a partitition. They numbered, on the plantations visited, from ten to twenty, and on the Coffin plantation, they are double, numbering twenty-three double houses, intended for forty-six families. The yards seemed to swarm with children, the negroes coupling at an early age.

Except on Sundays, these people do not take their meals at a family table, but each one takes his hominy, bread, or potatoes, sitting on the floor or a bench, and at his own time. They say their masters never allowed them any regular time for meals. Whoever, under our new system, is charged with their superintendence, should see that they attend more to the cleanliness of their persons and houses, and that, as in families of white people, they take their meals together at a table—habits to which they will be more disposed when they are provided with another change of clothing, and when better food is furnished and a proper hour assigned for meals.

Upon each plantation visited by me, familiar conversations were had with several laborers, more or less, as time permitted—sometimes inquiries made of them, as they collected in groups, as to what they desired us to do with and for them, with advice as to the course of sobriety and industry which it was for their interest to pursue under the new and strange circumstances in which they were now placed. Inquiries as to plantation economy, the culture of crops, the implements still remaining, the number of persons in all, and of field hands, and the rations issued, were made of the drivers, as they are called, answering as nearly as the two different systems of labor will permit to foremen on farms in the free States. There is one on each plantation—on the largest one visited, two. They still remained on each visited, and their names were noted. The business of the driver was to superintend the field-hands generally, and see that their tasks were performed fully and properly. He controlled them, subject to the master or overseer. He dealt out the rations. Another office belonged to him. He was required by the master or overseer, whenever he saw fit, to inflict corporal punishment upon the laborers; nor was he relieved from this office when the subject of discipline was his wife or children. In the absence of the master or overseer, he succeeded to much of their authority. As indicating his position of consequence, he was privileged with four suits of clothing a year, while only two were allowed to the laborers under him. It is evident, from some of the duties assigned to him, that he must have been a person of considerable judgment and knowledge of plantation economy, not differing essentially from that required of the foreman of a farm in the free States. He may be presumed to have known, in many cases, quite as much about the matters with which he was charged as the owner of the plantation, who often passed but a fractional part of his time upon it.

The driver, notwithstanding the dispersion of other laborers, quite generally remains on the plantation, as already stated. He still holds the keys of the granary, dealing out the rations of food, and with the same sense of responsibility as before. In one case, I found him in a controversy with a laborer to whom he was refusing his peck of corn, because of absence with his wife on another plantation when the corn was gathered,—it being gathered since the arrival of our army. The laborer protested warmly that he had helped to plant and hoe the corn, and was only absent as charged because of sickness. The driver appealed to me, as the only white man near, and learning from other laborers that the laborer was sick at the time of gathering, I advised the driver to give him his peck of corn, which he did accordingly. The fact is noted as indicating the present relation of the driver to the plantation, where he still retains something of his former authority.

This authority is, however, very essentially diminished. The main reason is, as he will assure you, that he has now no white man to back him. Other reasons may, however, concur. A class of laborers are generally disposed to be jealous of one of their own number promoted to be over them, and accordingly some negroes, evidently moved by this feeling, will tell you that the drivers ought now to work as field hands, and some field hands be drivers in their place. The driver has also been required to report delinquencies to the master or overseer, and upon their order to inflict corporal punishment. The laborers will, in some cases, say that he has been harder than he need to have been, while he will say that he did only what he was forced to do. The complainants who have suffered under the lash may be pardoned for not being sufficiently charitable to him who has unwillingly inflicted it, while, on the other hand, he has been placed in a dangerous position, where a hard nature, or self-interest, or dislike for the victim, might have tempted him to be more cruel than his position required. The truth, in proportions impossible for us in many cases to fix, may lie with both parties. I am, on the whole, inclined to believe that the past position of the driver and his valuable knowledge, both of the plantations and the laborers, when properly advised and controlled, may be made available in securing the productiveness of the plantations and the good of the laborers. It should be added that, in all cases, the drivers were found very ready to answer inquiries and communicate all information, and seemed desirous that the work of the season should be commenced.

There are also on the plantations other laborers, more intelligent than the average, such as the carpenter, the plowman, the religious leader, who may be called a preacher, a watchman or a helper,—the two latter being recognized officers in the churches of these people, and the helpers being aids to the watchman. These persons, having recognized positions among their fellows, either by virtue of superior knowledge or devotion, when properly approached by us, may be expected to have a beneficial influence on the more ignorant, and help to create that public opinion in favor of good conduct which, among the humblest as among the highest, is most useful. I saw many of very low intellectual development, but hardly any too low to be reached by civilizing influences, either coming directly from us or mediately through their brethren. And while I saw some who were sadly degraded, I met also others who were as fine specimens of human nature as one can ever expect to find.

Beside attendance on churches on Sundays, there are evening prayer-meetings on the plantations as often as once or twice a week, occupied with praying, singing, and exhortations. In some cases, the leader can read a hymn, having picked up his knowledge clandestinely, either from other negroes or from white children. Of the adults, about one-half, at least, are members of churches, generally the Baptist, although other denominations have communicants among them. In the Baptist Church on St. Helena Island, which I visited on the 22d January, there were a few pews for the proportionally small number of white attendants, and the much larger space devoted to benches for colored people. On one plantation there is a negro chapel, well adapted for the purpose, built by the proprietor, the late Mrs. Eustis, whose memory is cherished by the negroes, and some of whose sons are now loyal citizens of Massachusetts. I have heard among the negroes scarcely any profane swearing — not more than twice — a striking contrast with my experience among soldiers in the army.

It seemed a part of my duty to attend some of their religious meetings, and learn further about these people what could be derived from such a source. Their exhortations to personal piety were fervent, and, though their language was many times confused, at least to my ear, occasionally an important instruction or a felicitous expression could be recognized. In one case, a preacher of their own, commenting on the text, "Blessed are the meek," exhorted his brethren not to be "stout-minded." On one plantation on Ladies' Island, where some thirty negroes were gathered in the evening, I read passages of Scripture, and pressed on them their practical duties at the present time with reference to the good of themselves, their children, and their people. The passages read were the 1st and 23d Psalms; the 61st chapter of Isaiah, verses 1–4; the Beatitudes in the 5th chapter of Matthew; the 14th chapter of John's Gospel, and the 5th chapter of the Epistle of James. In substance, I told them that their masters had rebelled against the Government, and we had come to put down the rebellion; that we had now met them, and wanted to see what was best to do for them; that Mr. Lincoln, the President or Great Man at Washington, had the whole matter in charge, and was thinking what he could do for them; that the great trouble about doing anything for them was that their masters had always told us, and had made many people believe, that they were lazy, and would not work unless whipped to it; that Mr. Lincoln had sent us down here to see if it was so; that what they did was reported to him, or to men who would tell him; that where I came from all were free, both white and black; that we did not sell children or separate man and wife, but all had to work; that if they were to be free, they would have to work, and would be shut up or deprived of privileges if they did not; that this was a critical hour with them, and if they did not behave well now and respect our agents and appear willing to work, Mr. Lincoln would give up trying to do anything for them, and they must give up all hope for anything better, and their children and grand-children a hundred years hence would be worse off than they had been. I told them they must stick to their plantations and not run about and get scattered, and assured them that what their masters had told them of our intentions to carry them off to Cuba and sell them was a lie, and their masters knew it to be so, and we wanted them to stay on the plantations and raise cotton, and if they behaved well, they should have wages—small, perhaps, at first; that they should have better food, and not have their wives and children sold off; that their children should be taught to read and write, for which they might be willing to pay something; that by-and-by they would be as well off as the white people, and we would stand by them against their masters ever coming back to take them. The importance of exerting a good influence on each other, particularly on the younger men, who were rather careless and roving, was urged, as all would suffer in good repute from the bad deeds of a few. At Hilton Head, where I spoke to a meeting of two hundred, and there were facts calling for the counsel, the women were urged to keep away from the bad white men, who would ruin them. Remarks of a like character were made familiarly on the plantations to such groups as gathered about. At the Hilton Head meeting, a good-looking man, who had escaped from the southern part of Barnwell District, rose and said, with much feeling, that he and many others should do all they could by good conduct to prove what their masters said against them to be false, and to make Mr. Lincoln think better things of them. After the meeting closed, he desired to know if Mr. Lincoln was coming down here to see them, and he wanted me to give Mr. Lincoln his compliments, with his name, assuring the President that he would do all he could for him. The message was a little amusing, but it testified to the earnestness of the simple-hearted man. He had known Dr. Brisbane, who had been compelled some years since to leave the South because of his sympathy for slaves. The name of Mr. Lincoln was used in addressing them, as more likely to impress them than the abstract idea of government.

It is important to add that in no case have I attempted to excite them by insurrectionary appeals against their former masters, feeling that such a course might increase the trouble of organizing them into a peaceful and improving system, under a just and healthful temporary discipline; and besides that, it is a dangerous experiment to attempt the improvement of a class of men by appealing to their coarser nature. The better course toward making them our faithful allies, and therefore the constant enemies of the rebels, seemed to be to place before them the good things to be done for them and their children, and sometimes reading passages of Scripture appropriate to their lot, without, however, note or comment, never heard before by them, or heard only when wrested from their just interpretation; such, for instance, as the last chapter of St. James's Epistle, and the Glad Tidings of Isaiah: "I have come to preach deliverance to the captive." Thus treated and thus educated, they may be hoped to become useful coadjutors, and the unconquerable foes of the fugitive rebels.

There are some vices charged upon these people which deserve examination. Notwithstanding their religious professions, in some cases more emotional than practical, the marriage relation, or what answers for it, is not, in many instances, held very sacred by them. The men, it is said, sometimes leave one wife and take another,—something likely to happen in any society where it is permitted or not forbidden by a stern public opinion, and far more likely to happen under laws which do not recognize marriage, and dissolve what answers for it by forced separations, dictated by the mere pecuniary interest of others. The women, it is said, are easily persuaded by white men,—a facility readily accounted for by the power of the master over them, whose solicitation was equivalent to a command, and against which the husband or father was powerless to protect, and increased also by the degraded condition in which they have been placed, where they have been apt to regard what ought to be a disgrace as a compliment, when they were approached by a paramour of superior condition and race. Yet often the dishonor is felt, and the woman, on whose several children her master's features are impressed, and through whose veins his blood flows, has sadly confessed it with an instinctive blush. The grounds of this charge, so far as they may exist, will be removed, as much as in communities of our own race, by a system which shall recognize and enforce the marriage relation among them, protect them against the solicitations of white men as much as law can, still more by putting them in relations were they will be inspired with self-respect and a consciousness of their rights, and taught by a pure and plain-spoken Christianity.

In relation to the veracity of these people, so far as my relations with them have extended, they have appeared, as a class, to intend to tell the truth. Their manner, as much as among white men, bore instinctive evidence of this intention. Their answers to inquiries relative to the management of the plantations have a general concurrence. They make no universal charges of cruelty against their masters. They will say, in some cases, that their own was a very kind one, but another one in that neighborhood was cruel. On St. Helena Island they spoke kindly of "the good William Fripp," as they called him, and of Dr. Clarence Fripp; but they all denounced the cruelty of Alvira Fripp, recounting his inhuman treatment of both men and women. Another concurrence is worthy of note. On the plantations visited, it appeared from the statements of the laborers themselves, that there were, on an average, about 133 pounds of cotton produced to the acre, and five acres of cotton and corn cultivated to a hand, the culture of potatoes not being noted. An article of the American Agriculturist, published in Turner's Cotton Manual, pp. 132, 133, relative to the culture of Sea Island Cotton, on the plantation of John H. Townsend, states that the land is cultivated in the proportion of 7-12th cotton, 3-12ths corn, and 2-12ths potatoes—in all, less than six acres to a hand—and the average yield of cotton per acre is 135 pounds. I did not take the statistics of the culture of potatoes, but about five acres are planted with them on the smaller plantations, and twenty, or even thirty, on the larger; and the average amount of land to each hand, planted with potatoes, should be added to the five acres of cotton and corn, and thus results not differing substantially are reached in both cases. Thus the standard publications attest the veracity and accuracy of these laborers.

Again, there can be no more delicate and responsible position, involving honesty and skill, than that of pilot. For this purpose, these people are every day employed to aid our military and naval operations in navigating these sinuous channels. They were used in the recent reconnoisance in the direction of Savannah; and the success of the affair at Port Royal Ferry depended on the fidelity of a pilot, William, without the aid of whom, or of one like him, it could not have been undertaken. Further information on this point may be obtained of the proper authorities here. These services are not, it is true, in all respects, illustrative of the quality of veracity, but they involve kindred virtues not likely to exist without it.

It is proper, however, to state that expressions are sometimes heard from persons who have not considered these people thoughtfully, to the effect that their word is not to be trusted, and these persons, nevertheless, do trust them, and act upon their statements. There may, however, be some color for such expressions. These laborers, like all ignorant people, have an ill-regulated reason, too much under the control of the imagination. Therefore, where they report the number of soldiers, or relate facts where there is room for conjecture, they are likely to be extravagant, and you must scrutinize their reports. Still, except among the thoroughly dishonest,—no more numerous among them than in other races,—there will be found a colorable basis for their statements, enough to show their honest intention to speak truly.

It is true also that you will find them too willing to express feelings which will please you. This is most natural. All races, as well as all animals, have their appropriate means of self-defence, and where the power to use physical force to defend one's self is taken away, the weaker animal, or man, or race, resorts to cunning and duplicity. Whatever habits of this kind may appear in these people are directly traceable to the well-known features of their past condition, without involving any essential proneness to deception in the race, further than may be ascribed to human nature. Upon this point, special inquiries have been made of the Superintendent at Hilton Head, who is brought in direct daily association with them, and whose testimony, truthful as he is, is worth far more than that of those who have had less nice opportunities of observation, and Mr. Lee certifies to the results here presented. Upon the question of the disposition of these people to work, there are different reports, varied somewhat by the impression an idle or an industrious laborer, brought into immediate relation with the witness, may have made on the mind. In conversations with them, they uniformly answered to assurances that if free they must work, "Yes, massa, we must work to live; that's the law"; and expressing an anxiety that the work of the plantations was not going on. At Hilton Head, they are ready to do for Mr. Lee, the judicious Superintendent, whatever is desired. Hard words and epithets are, however, of no use in managing them, and other parties for whose service they are specially detailed, who do not understand or treat them properly, find some trouble in making their labor available, as might naturally be expected. In collecting cotton, it is sometimes, as I am told, difficult to get them together, when wanted for work. There may be something in this, particularly among the young men. I have observed them a good deal; and though they often do not work to much advantage,—a dozen doing sometimes what one or two stout and well-trained Northern laborers would do, and though less must always be expected of persons native to this soil than those bred in Northern latitudes, and under more bracing air,—I have not been at all impressed with their general indolence. As servants, oarsmen, and carpenters, I have seen them working faithfully and with a will. There are some peculiar circumstances in their condition, which no one who assumes to sit in judgment upon them must overlook. They are now, for the first time, freed from the restraint of a master, and like children whose guardian or teacher is absent for the day, they may quite naturally enjoy an interval of idleness. No system of labor for them, outside of the camps, has been begun, and they have had nothing to do except to bale the cotton when bagging was furnished, and we all know that men partially employed are, if anything, less disposed to do the little assigned them than they are to perform the full measure which belongs to them in regular life, the virtue of the latter case being supported by habit. At the camps, they are away from their accustomed places of labor, and have not been so promptly paid as could be desired, and are exposed to the same circumstances which often dispose soldiers to make as little exertion as possible. In the general chaos which prevails, and before the inspirations of labor have been set before them by proper superintendents and teachers who understand their disposition, and show by their conduct an interest in their welfare, no humane or reasonable man would subject them to austere criticism, or make the race responsible for the delinquencies of an idle person, who happened to be brought particularly under his own observation. Not thus would we have ourselves or our own race judged; and the judgment which we would not have meted to us, let us not measure to others.

Upon the best examination of these people, and a comparison of the evidence of trustworthy persons, I believe that when properly organized, and with proper motives set before them, they will, as freemen, be as industrious as any race of men are likely to be in this climate.

The notions of the sacredness of property as held by these people have sometimes been the subject of discussion here. It is reported they have taken things left in their masters' houses. It was wise to prevent this, and even where it had been done to compel a restoration, at least of expensive articles, lest they should be injured by speedily acquiring, without purchase, articles above their condition. But a moment's reflection will show that it was the most natural thing for them to do. They had been occupants of the estates; had had these things more or less in charge, and when the former owners had left, it was easy for them to regard their title to the abandoned property as better than that of strangers. Still, it is not true that they have, except as to very simple articles, as soap or dishes, generally availed themselves of such property. It is also stated that in camps where they have been destitute of clothing, they have stolen from each other, but the Superintendents are of opinion that they would not have done this if already well provided. Besides, those familiar with large bodies collected together, like soldiers in camp life, also know how often these charges of mutual pilfering are made among them, often with great injustice. It should be added, to complete the statement, that the agents who have been intrusted with the collection of cotton have reposed confidence in the trustworthiness of the laborers, committing property to their charge—a confidence not found to have been misplaced.

To what extent these laborers desire to be free, and to serve us still further in putting down the rebellion, has been a subject of examination. The desire to be free has been strongly expressed, particularly among the more intelligent and adventurous. Every day, almost, adds a fresh tale of escapes, both solitary and in numbers, conducted with a courage, a forecast, and a skill, worthy of heroes. But there are other apparent features in their disposition which it would be untruthful to conceal. On the plantations, I often found a disposition to evade the inquiry whether they wished to be free or slaves; and though a preference for freedom was expressed, it was rarely in the passionate phrases which would come from an Italian peasant. The secluded and monotonous life of a plantation, with strict discipline and ignorance enforced by law and custom, is not favorable to the development of the richer sentiments, though even there they find at least a stunted growth, irrepressible as they are. The inquiry was often answered in this way: "The white man do what he pleases with us; we are yours now, massa." One, if I understood his broken words rightly, said that he did not care about being free, if he only had a good master. Others said they would like to be free, but they wanted a white man for a "protector." All of proper age, when inquired of, expressed a desire to have their children taught to read and write, and to learn themselves. On this point, they showed more earnestness than on any other. When asked if they were willing to fight, in case we needed them, to keep their masters from coming back, they would seem to shrink from that, saying that "black men have been kept down so like dogs that they would run before white men." At the close of the first week's observation, I almost concluded that on the plantation there was but little earnest desire for freedom, and scarcely any willingness for its sake to encounter white men. But as showing the importance of not attempting to reach general conclusions too hastily, another class of facts came to my notice the second week. I met then some more intelligent, who spoke with profound earnestness of their desire to be free, and how they had longed to see this day. Other facts, connected with the military and naval operations, were noted. At the recent reconnoisance toward Pulaski, pilots of this class stood well under the fire, and were not reluctant to the service. When a district of Ladies' Island was left exposed, they voluntarily took such guns as they could procure, and stood sentries. Also at North Edisto, where the colony is collected under the protection of our gunboats, they armed themselves and drove back the rebel cavalry. An officer here high in command reported to me some of these facts, which had been officially communicated to him. The suggestion may be pertinent that the persons in question are divisible into two classes. Those who, by their occupation, have been accustomed to independent labor, and schooled in some sort of self-reliance, are more developed in this direction; while others, who have been bound to the routine of plantation life, and kept more strictly under surveillance, are but little awakened. But even among these last there has been, under the quickening inspiration of present events, a rapid development, indicating that the same feeling is only latent.

There is another consideration which must not be omitted. Many of these people have still but little confidence in us, anxiously looking to see what is to be our disposition of them, It is a mistake to suppose that, separated from the world, never having read a Northern book or newspaper relative to them, or talked with a Northern man expressing the sentiments prevalent in his region, they are universally and with entire confidence welcoming us as their deliverers. Here, as everywhere else, where our army has met them, they have been assured by their masters that we were going to carry them off to Cuba. There is probably not a rebel master, from the Potomac to the Gulf, who has not repeatedly made this assurance to his slaves. No matter what his religious vows may have been, no matter what his professed honor as a gentleman, he has not shrunk from the reiteration of this falsehood. Never was there a people, as all who know them will testify, more attached to familiar places than they. Be their home a cabin, and not even that cabin their own, they still cling to it. The reiteration could not fail to have had some effect on a point on which they were so sensitive. Often it must have been met with unbelief or great suspicion of its truth. It was also balanced by the consideration that their masters would remove them into the interior, and perhaps to a remote region, and separate their families, about as bad as being taken to Cuba, and they felt more inclined to remain on the plantations, and take their chances with us. They have told me that they reasoned in this way. But in many cases they fled at the approach of our army. Then one or two bolder returning, the rest were reässured and came back. Recently, the laborers at Parry Island, seeing some schooners approaching suspiciously, commenced gathering their little effects rapidly together, and were about to run, when they were quieted by some of our teachers coming, in whom they had confidence. In some cases, their distrust has been increased by the bad conduct of some irresponsible white men, of which, for the honor of human nature, it is not best to speak more particularly. On the whole, their confidence in us has been greatly increased by the treatment they have received, which, in spite of many individual cases of injury less likely to occur under the stringent orders recently issued from the naval and military authorities, has been generally kind and humane. But the distrust which to a greater or less extent may have existed on our arrival, renders necessary, if we would keep them faithful allies, and not informers to the enemy, the immediate adoption of a system which shall be a pledge of our protection and of our permanent interest in their welfare.

The manner of the laborers toward us has been kind and deferential, doing for us such good offices as were in their power, as guides, pilots, or in more personal service, inviting us on the plantations to lunch of hominy and milk, or potatoes, touching the hat in courtesy, and answering politely such questions as were addressed to them. If there have been exceptions to this rule, it was in the case of those whose bearing did not entitle them to the civility.

Passing from general phases of character or present disposition, the leading facts in relation to the plantations and the mode of rendering them useful and determining what is best to be done, come next in order.

The laborers on St. Helena and Ladies' Islands very generally remain on their respective plantations. This fact, arising partially from local attachment and partially because they can thus secure their allowance of corn, is important, as it will facilitate their reörganization. Some are absent, temporarily visiting a wife, or relative, on another plantation, and returning periodically for their rations. The disposition to roam, so far as it exists, mainly belongs to the younger people. On Port Royal and Hilton Head Islands, there is a much greater dispersion, due in part to their having been the scene of more active military movements, and in part to the taking in greater measure on these islands of the means of subsistence from the plantations. When the work recommences, however, there is not likely to be any indisposition to return to them.

The statistics with regard to the number of laborers, field hands, acres planted to cotton and corn, are not presented as accurate statements, but only as reasonable approximations, which may be of service.

The highest number of people on any plantation visited was on Coffin's, where there are 260. Those on the plantation of Dr. Jenkins number 130; on that of the Eustis estate, 120; and the others, from 80 to 38. The average number on each is 81. The field hands range generally from one-third to one-half of the number, the rest being house servants, old persons, and children. About five acres of cotton and corn are planted to a hand; and to potatoes, about five acres in all were devoted on the smaller plantations, and from twenty to thirty on the larger.

The number of pounds in a bale of ginned cotton ranges from 300 to 400 — the average number being not far from 345 pounds per bale. The average yield per acre on fifteen plantations was about 133 pounds.

The material for compost is gathered in the periods of most leisure — often in July and August, after the cultivation of the cotton plant is ended, and before the picking has commenced. Various materials are used, but quite generally mud and the coarse marsh grass, which abounds on the creeks near the plantations, are employed. The manure is carted upon the land in January and February, and left in heaps, two or three cart-loads on each task, to be spread at the time of listing. The land, by prevailing custom, lies fallow a year. The cotton and corn are planted in elevated rows or beds. The next step is the listing, done with the hoe, and making the bed where the alleys were at the previous raising of the crop, and the alleys being made where the beds were before. In this process, half the old bed is hauled into the alley on the one side, and the other half into the alley on the other. This work is done mainly in February, being commenced sometimes the last of January. A "task" is

105 feet square, and contains twenty-one or twenty-two beds or rows. Each laborer is required to list a task and a half, or if the land is moist and heavy, a task and five or seven beds, say one-fourth or three-eighths of an acre.

The planting of cotton commences about the 20th or last of March, and of corn about the same time or earlier. It is continued through April, and by some planters it is not begun till April. The seeds are deposited in the beds, a foot or a foot and a half apart on light land, and two feet apart on heavy land, and five or ten seeds left in a place. After the plant is growing, the stalks are thinned so as to leave together two on high land and one on low or rich land. The hoeing of the early cotton begins about the time that the planting of the late has ended. The plant is cultivated with the hoe and plow during May, June and July, keeping the weeds down and thinning the stalks. The picking commences the last of August. The cotton being properly dried in the sun, is then stored in houses, ready to be ginned. The ginning, or cleaning the fibre from the seed, is done either by gins operated by steam, or by the well-known foot-gins — the latter turning out about 30 pounds of ginned cotton per day, and worked by one person, assisted by another, who picks out the specked and yellow cotton. The steam-engine carries one or more gins, each turning out 300 pounds per day, and requiring eight or ten hands to tend the engine and gins, more or less, according to the number of the gins. The foot-gins are still more used than the gins operated by steam, — the latter being used mainly on the largest plantations, on which both kinds are sometimes employed. I have preserved notes of the kind and number of gins used on the plantations visited, but it is unnecessary to give them here. Both kinds can be run entirely by the laborers, and after this year, the ginning should be done entirely here — among other reasons, to avoid transportation of the seed, which makes nearly three-fourths of the weight of the unginned cotton, and to preserve in better condition the seed required for planting.

The allowance of clothing to the field hands in this district has been two suits per year, one for summer and another for winter. That of food has been mainly vegetable — a peck of corn a week to each hand, with meat only in June, when the work is hardest, and at Christmas. No meat was allowed in June, on some plantations, while on a few, more liberal, it was dealt out occasionally—as once a fortnight, or once a month. On a few, molasses was given at intervals. Children, varying with their ages, were allowed from two to six quarts of corn per week. The diet is more exclusively vegetable here than almost anywhere in the rebellious regions, and in this respect should be changed. It should be added, that there are a large quantity of oysters available for food in proper seasons.

Besides the above rations, the laborers were allowed each to cultivate a small patch of ground, about a quarter of an acre, for themselves, when their work for their master was done. On this, corn and potatoes, chiefly the former, were planted. The corn was partly eaten by themselves, thus supplying in part the deficiency in rations; but it was, to a great extent, fed to a pig, or chickens, each hand being allowed to keep a pig and chickens or ducks, but not geese or turkeys. With the proceeds of the pig and chickens, generally sold to the masters, and at pretty low rates, extra clothing, coffee, sugar, and that necessary of life with these people, as they think, tobacco, were bought.

In the report thus far, such facts in the condition of the territory now occupied by the forces of the United States have been noted as seemed to throw light on what could be done to reörganize the laborers, prepare them to become sober and self-supporting citizens, and secure the successful culture of a cotton-crop, now so necessary to be contributed to the markets of the world. It will appear from them that these people are naturally religious and simple-hearted—attached to the places where they have lived, still adhering to them both from a feeling of local attachment and self-interest in securing the means of subsistence; that they have the knowledge and experience requisite to do all the labor, from the preparation of the ground for planting until the cotton is baled, ready to be exported; that they, or the great mass of them, are disposed to labor, with proper inducements thereto; that they lean upon white men, and desire their protection, and could, therefore, under a wise system, be easily brought under subordination; that they are susceptible to the higher considerations, as duty, and the love of offspring, and are not in any way inherently vicious, their defects coming from their peculiar condition in the past or present, and not from constitutional proneness to evil beyond what may be attributed to human nature; that they have among them natural chiefs, either by virtue of religious leadership or superior intelligence, who, being first addressed, may exert a healthful influence on the rest. In a word, that, in spite of their condition, reputed to be worse here than in many other parts of the rebellious region, there are such features in their life and character, that the opportunity is now offered to us to make of them, partially in this generation, and fully in the next, a happy, industrious, law-abiding, free and Christian people, if we have but the courage and patience to accept it. If this be the better view of them and their possibilities, I will say that I have come to it after anxious study of all peculiar circumstances in their lot and character, and after anxious conference with reflecting minds here, who are prosecuting like inquiries, not overlooking what, to a casual spectator, might appear otherwise, and granting what is likely enough, that there are those among them whose characters, by reason of bad nature or treatment, are set, and not admitting of much improvement. And I will submit further, that, in common fairness and common charity, when, by the order of Providence, an individual or a race is committed to our care, the better view is entitled to be first practically applied. If this one shall be accepted and crowned with success, history will have the glad privilege of recording that this wicked and unprovoked rebellion was not without compensations most welcome to our race.

What, then, should be the true system of administration here?

It has been proposed to lease the plantations and the people upon them. To this plan there are two objections—each conclusive. In the first place, the leading object of the parties bidding for leases would be to obtain a large immediate revenue—perhaps to make a fortune in a year or two. The solicitations of doubtful men, offering the highest price, would impose on the leasing power a stern duty of refusal, to which it ought not unnecessarily to be subjected. Far better a system which shall not invite such men to harass the leasing power, or excite expectations of a speedy fortune, to be derived from the labor of this people. Secondly: No man, not even the best of men, charged with the duties which ought to belong to the guardians of these people, should be put in a position where there would be such a conflict between his humanity and his self-interest—his desire, on the one hand, to benefit the laborer, and, on the other, the too often stronger desire to reap a large revenue—perhaps to restore broken fortunes in a year or two. Such a system is beset with many of the worst vices of the slave system, with one advantage in favor of the latter, that it is for the interest of the planter to look to permanent results. Let the history of British East India, and of all communities where a superior race has attempted to build up speedy fortunes on the labor of an inferior race occupying another region, be remembered, and no just man will listen to the proposition of leasing, fraught as it is with such dangerous consequences. Personal confidence forbids me to report the language of intense indignation which has been expressed against it here by some occupying high places of command, as also by others who have come here for the special purpose of promoting the welfare of these laborers. Perhaps it might yield to the treasury a larger immediate revenue, but it would be sure to spoil the country and its people in the end. The Government should be satisfied if the products of the territory may be made sufficient for a year or two to pay the expenses of administration and superintendence, and the inauguration of a beneficent system which will settle a great social question, ensure the sympathies of foreign nations, now wielded against us, and advance the civilization of the age.

The better course would be to appoint superintendents for each large plantation, and one for two or three smaller combined, compensated with a good salary, say $1,000 per year, selected with reference to peculiar qualifications, and as carefully as one would choose a guardian for his children, clothed with an adequate power to enforce a paternal discipline, to require a proper amount of labor, cleanliness, sobriety, and better habits of life, and generally to promote the moral and intellectual culture of the wards, with such other inducements, if there be any, placed before the superintendent as shall inspire him to constant efforts to prepare them for useful and worthy citizenship. To quicken and ensure the fidelity of the superintendents, there should a director-general or governor, who shall visit the plantations, and see that they are discharging these duties, and, if necessary, he should be aided by others in the duty of visitation. This officer should be invested with liberal powers over all persons within his jurisdiction, so as to protect the blacks from each other and from white men, being required in most important cases to confer with the military authorities in punishing offences. His proposed duties indicate that he should be a man of the best ability and character: better if he have already, by virtue of public services, a hold on the public confidence. Such an arrangement is submitted as preferable for the present to any cumbersome territorial government.

The laborers themselves, no longer slaves of their former masters, or of the Government, but as yet in large numbers unprepared for the full privileges of citizens, are to be treated with sole reference to such preparation. No effort is to be spared to work upon their better nature and the motives which come from it—the love of wages, of offspring, and family, the desire of happiness, and the obligations of religion. And when these fail,—and fail they will, in some cases,—we must not hesitate to resort, not to the lash, for as from the department of war so also from the department of labor, it must be banished, but to the milder and more effective punishments of deprivation of privileges, isolation from family and society, the workhouse, or even the prison. The laborers are to be assured at the outset that parental and conjugal relations among them are to be protected and enforced; that children, and all others desiring, are to be taught; that they will receive wages; and that a certain just measure of work, with reference to the ability to perform it, if not willingly rendered, is to be required of all. The work, so far as the case admits, shall be assigned in proper tasks, the standard being what a healthy person of average capacity can do, for which a definite sum is to be paid. The remark may perhaps be pertinent, that, whatever may have been the case with women or partially disabled persons, my observations, not yet sufficient to decide the point, have not impressed me with the conviction that healthy persons, if they had been provided with an adequate amount of food, and that animal in due proportion, could be said to have been overworked heretofore on these islands, the main trouble having been that they have not been so provided, and have not had the motives which smooth labor. Notwithstanding the frequent and severe chastisements which have been employed here in exacting labor, they have failed, and naturally enough, of their intended effects. Human beings are made up of so much more of spirit than of muscle, that compulsory labor, enforced by physical pain, will not exceed or equal, in the long run, voluntary labor with just inspirations; and the same law in less degree may be seen in the difference between the value of a whipped and jaded beast, and one well disciplined and kindly treated.

What should be the standard of wages where none have heretofore been paid, is less easy to determine. It should be graduated with reference to the wants of the laborer and the ability of the employer or Government; and this ability being determined by the value of the products of the labor, and the most that should be expected being, that for a year or two the system should not be a burden on the Treasury. Taking into consideration the cost of food and clothing, medical attendance and extras, supposing that the laborer would require rations of pork or beef, meal, coffee, sugar, molasses and tobacco, and that he would work 300 days in the year, he should receive about forty cents a day in order to enable him to lay up $30 a year; and each healthy woman could do about equally well. Three hundred days in a year is, perhaps, too high an estimate of working days, when we consider the chances of sickness and days when, by reason of storms and other causes, there would be no work. It is assumed that the laborer is not to pay rent for the small house tenanted by him. This sum, when the average number of acres cultivated by a hand, and the average yield per acre are considered with reference to market prices, or when the expense of each laborer to his former master, the interest on his assumed value and on the value of the land worked by him,—these being the elements of what it has cost the master before making a profit,—are computed, the Government could afford to pay, leaving an ample margin to meet the cost of the necessary implements, as well as of superintendence and administration. The figures on which this estimate is based are at the service of the Department if desired. It must also be borne in mind that the plantations will in the end be carried on more scientifically and cheaply than before, the plough taking very much the place of the hoe, and other implements being introduced to facilitate industry and increase the productive power of the soil.

It being important to preserve all former habits which are not objectionable, the laborer should have his patch of ground on which to raise corn or vegetables for consumption or sale.

As a part of the plan proposed, missionaries will be needed to address the religious element of a race so emotional in their nature, exhorting to all practical virtues, and inspiring the laborers with a religious zeal for faithful labor, the good nurture of their children, and for clean and healthful habits. The benevolence of the Free States, now being directed hither, will gladly provide these. The Government should, however, provide some teachers specially devoted to teaching reading, writing and arithmetic, say some twenty-five, for the territory now occupied by our forces, and private benevolence might even be relied on for these.

The plan proposed is, of course, not presented as an ultimate result: far from it. It contemplates a paternal discipline for the time being, intended for present use only, with the prospect of better things in the future. As fast as the laborers show themselves fitted for all the privileges of citizens, they should be dismissed from the system and allowed to follow any employment they please, and where they please. They should have the power to acquire the fee simple of land, either with the proceeds of their labor or as a reward of special merit; and it would be well to quicken their zeal for good behavior by proper recognitions. I shall not follow these suggestions, as to the future, further, contenting myself with indicating what is best to be done at once with a class of fellow-beings now thrown on our protection, entitled to be recognized as freemen, but for whose new condition the former occupants of the territory have diligently labored to unfit them.

But whatever is thought best to be done, should be done at once. A system ought to have been commenced with the opening of the year. Beside that, demoralization increases with delay. The months of January and February are the months for preparing the ground by manuring and listing, and the months of March and April are for planting. Already, important time has passed, and in a very few weeks it will be too late to prepare for a crop, and too late to assign useful work to the laborers for a year to come. I implore the immediate intervention of your Department to avert the calamities which must ensue from a further postponement.

There is another precaution most necessary to be taken. As much as possible, persons enlisted in the army and navy should be kept separate from these people. The association produces an unhealthy excitement in the latter, and there are other injurious results to both parties which it is unnecessary to particularize. In relation to this matter, I had an interview with the Flag-Officer, Com. Dupont, which resulted in an order that "no boats from any of the ships of the squadron can be permitted to land anywhere but at Bay Point and Hilton Head, without a pass from the Fleet Captain," and requiring the commanding officers of the vessels to give special attention to all intercourse between the men under their command and the various plantations in their vicinity. Whatever can be accomplished to that end by this humane and gallant officer, who superadds to skill and courage in his profession the liberal views of a statesman, will not be left undone. The suggestion should also be made that, when employment is given to this people, some means should be taken to enable them to obtain suitable goods at fair rates, and precautions taken to prevent the introduction of ardent spirits among them.

A loyal citizen of Massachusetts, Mr. Frederick A. Eustis, has recently arrived here. He is the devisee in a considerable amount under the will of the late Mrs. Eustis, who owned the large estate on Ladies' Island, and also another at Pocotaligo, the latter not yet in possession of our forces. The executors are rebels, and reside at Charleston. Mr. Eustis has as yet received no funds by reason of the devise. There are two other loyal devisees and some other devisees resident in rebellious districts, and the latter are understood to have received dividends. Mr. Eustis is a gentleman of humane and liberal views, and, accepting the present condition of things, desires that the people on these plantations should not be distinguished from their brethren on others, but equally admitted to their better fortunes. The circumstances of this case, though of a personal character, may furnish a useful precedent. With great pleasure and confidence, I recommend that this loyal citizen be placed in charge of the plantation on Ladies' Island, which he is willing to accept—the questions of property and rights under the will being reserved for subsequent determination.

A brief statement in relation to the laborers collected at the camps at Hilton Head and Beaufort may be desirable. At both places, they are under the charge of the Quartermaster's Department. At Hilton Head, Mr. Barnard K. Lee, Jr., of Boston, is the Superintendent, assisted by Mr. J. D. McMath of Alleghany City, Penn., both civilians. The appointment of Mr. Lee is derived from Captain R. Saxton, Chief Quartermaster of the Expeditionary Corps, a humane officer, who is deeply interested in this matter. The number at this camp are about 600, the registered number under Mr. Lee being 472, of which 137 are on the pay-roll. Of these 472, 279 are fugitives from the main land, or other points, still held by the rebels; 77 are from Hilton Head Island; 62 from the adjacent island of Pinckney; 38 from St. Helena; 8 from Port Royal; 7 from Spring, and one from Daufuskie. Of the 472, the much larger number, it will be seen, have sought refuge from the places now held by rebels; while the greater proportion of the remainder came in at an early period, before they considered themselves safe elsewhere. Since the above figures were given, forty-eight more, all from one plantation, and under the lead of the driver, came in together from the main land. Mr. Lee was appointed November 10th last, with instructions to assure the laborers that they would be paid a reasonable sum for their services, not yet fixed. They were contented with the assurance, and a quantity of blankets and clothing captured of the rebels was issued to them without charge. About December 1st, an order was given that carpenters should be paid $8 per month, and other laborers $5 per month. Women and children were fed without charge, the women obtaining washing and receiving the pay, in some cases in considerable sums, not, however, heretofore, very available, as there was no clothing for women for sale here. It will be seen that, under the order, laborers, particularly those with families, have been paid with sufficient liberality. There were 63 laborers on the pay-roll on December 1st, and $101.50 were paid to them for the preceding month. On January 1st, there were for the preceding month 127 on the pay-roll, entitled to $468.59. On February 1st, there were for the preceding month 137 on the pay-roll, entitled to something more than for the month of January; making in all due them not far from $1000. This delay of payment, due, it is stated, to a deficiency of small currency, has made the laborers uneasy, and affected the disposition to work.

On January 18th, a formal order was issued by General Sherman, regulating the rate of wages, varying from $12 to $8 per month for mechanics, and from $8 to $4 for other laborers. Under it, each laborer is to have, in addition, a ration of food. But from the monthly pay are to be deducted rations for his family, if here, and clothing both for himself and family. Commodious barracks have been erected for these people, and a guard protects their quarters.

I have been greatly impressed by the kindness and good sense of Mr. Lee and his assistant, in their discipline of these people. The lash, let us give thanks, is banished at last. No coarse words or profanity are used toward them. There has been less than a case of discipline a week, and the delinquent, if a male, is sometimes made to stand on a barrel, or, if a woman, is put in a dark room, and such discipline has proved successful. The only exception, if any, is in the case of one woman, and the difficulty there was conjugal jealousy, she protesting that she was compelled by her master, against her will, to live with the man.

There is scarcely any profanity among them, more than one-half of the adults being members of churches. Their meetings are held twice or three times on Sundays, also on the evenings of Tuesday, Thursday and Friday. They are conducted with fervent devotion by themselves alone or in presence of a white clergyman, when the services of one are procurable. They close with what is called "a glory shout," one joining hands with another, together in couples singing a verse and beating time with the foot. A fastidious religionist might object to this exercise; but being in accordance with usage, and innocent enough in itself, it is not open to exception. As an evidence of the effects of the new system in inspiring self-reliance, it should be noted that the other evening they called a meeting of their own accord, and voted, the motion being regularly made and put, that it was now but just that they should provide the candles for their meetings, hitherto provided by the Government. A collection was taken at a subsequent meeting, and $2.48 was the result. The incident may be trivial, but it justifies a pleasing inference. No school, it is to be regretted, has yet been started, except one on Sundays, but the call for reading books is daily made by the laborers. The suggestion of Mr. Lee, in which I most heartily concur, should not be omitted—that with the commencement of the work on the plantations, the laborers should be distributed upon them, having regard to the family relations and the places whence they come.

Of the number and condition of the laborers at Beaufort, less accurate information was attainable, and fewer statistics than could be desired. They have not, till within a few days, had a General Superintendent, but have been under the charge of persons detailed for the purpose from the army. I saw one whose manner and language toward them was, to say the least, not elevating. A new Quartermaster of the post has recently commenced his duties, and a better order of things is expected. He has appointed as Superintendent Mr. Wm. Harding, a citizen of Daufuskie Island. An enrollment has commenced, but is not yet finished. There are supposed to be about six hundred at Beaufort. The number has been larger, but some have already returned to the plantations in our possession from which they came. At this point, the Rev. Solomon Peck, of Roxbury, Mass., has done great good in preaching to them and protecting them from the depredations of white men. He has established a school for the children, in which are sixty pupils, ranging in age from six to fifteen years. They are rapidly learning their letters and simple reading. The teachers are of the same race with the taught, of ages respectively of twenty, thirty, and fifty years. The name of one is John Milton. A visit to the school leaves a remarkable impression. One sees there those of pure African blood, and others ranging through the lighter shades, and among them brunettes of the fairest features. I taught several of the children their letters for an hour or two, and during the recess heard the three teachers, at their own request, recite their spelling-lessons of words of one syllable, and read two chapters of Matthew. It seemed to be a morning well spent. Nor have the efforts of Dr. Peck been confined to this point. He has preached at Cat, Cane and Ladies' Island, anticipating all other white clergymen, and on Sunday, February 2d, at the Baptist Church on St. Helena, to a large congregation, where his ministrations have been attended with excellent effects. On my visits to St. Helena, I found that no white clergyman had been there since our military occupation began, that the laborers were waiting for one, and there was a demoralization at some points which timely words might arrest. I may be permitted to state, that it was at my own suggestion that he made the appointment on this island. I cannot forbear to give a moment's testimony to the nobility of character displayed by this venerable man. Of mild and genial temperament, equally earnest and sensible, enjoying the fruits of culture, and yet not dissuaded by them from the humblest toil, having reached an age when most others would have declined the duty, and left it to be discharged by younger men; of narrow means, and yet in the main defraying his own expenses, this man of apostolic faith and life, to whose labors both hemispheres bear witness, left his home to guide and comfort this poor and shepherdless flock; and to him belongs, and ever will belong, the distinguished honor of being the first minister of Christ to enter the field which our arms had opened.

The Rev. Mansfield French, whose mission was authenticated and approved by the Government, prompted by benevolent purposes of his own, and in conference with others in the city of New York, has been here two weeks, during which time he has been industriously occupied in examining the state of the islands and their population, in conferring with the authorities, and laying the foundation of beneficent appliances with reference to their moral, educational, and material wants. These, having received the sanction of officers in command, he now returns to commend to the public, and the Government will derive important information from his report. Beside other things, he proposes, with the approval of the authorities here, to secure authority to introduce women of suitable experience and ability, who shall give industrial instruction to those of their own sex among these people, and who, visiting from dwelling to dwelling, shall strive to improve their household life, and give such counsels as women can best communicate to women. All civilizing influences like these should be welcomed here, and it cannot be doubted that many noble hearts among the women of the land will volunteer for the service.

There are some material wants of this territory requiring immediate attention. The means of subsistence have been pretty well preserved on the plantations on St. Helena; so also on that part of Ladies' adjacent to St. Helena. But on Port Royal Island, and that part of Ladies' near to it, destitution has commenced, and will, unless provision is made, become very great. Large amounts of corn for forage, in quantities from fifty to four or five hundred bushels from a plantation, have been taken to Beaufort. On scarcely any within this district is there enough to last beyond April, whereas it is needed till August. On others, it will last only two or three weeks, and on some it is entirely exhausted. It is stated that the forage was taken because no adequate supply was at hand, and requisitions for it were not seasonably answered. The further taking of the corn in this way has now been forbidden; but the Government must be prepared to meet the exigency which it has itself created. It should be remembered that this is not a grain-exporting region, corn being produced in moderate crops only for consumption. Similar destitution will take place on other islands, from the same cause, unless provision is made.

The horses, mules and oxen, in large numbers, have been taken to Beaufort and Hilton Head as means of transportation. It is presumed that they, or most of them, are no longer needed for that purpose, and that they will be returned to those who shall have charge of the plantations. Cattle to the number of a hundred, and in some cases less, have been taken from a plantation and slaughtered, to furnish fresh beef for the army. Often cattle have been killed by irresponsible foraging parties, acting without compêtent authority. There can be no doubt that the army and navy have been in great want of the variation of the rations of salt beef or pork; but it also deserves much consideration, if the plantations are to be permanently worked, how much of a draught they can sustain.

The garden seeds have been pretty well used up, and I inclose a desirable list furnished me by a gentleman whose perience enables him to designate those adapted to the soil, and useful too for army supplies. The general cultivation of the islands also requires the sending of a quantity of ploughs and hoes.

It did not seem a part of my duty to look specially after matters which had been safely entrusted to others; but it is pleasing, from such observation as was casually made, to testify that Lieutenant-Colonel William H. Reynolds, who was charged with the preservation of the cotton and other confiscated property, notwithstanding many difficulties in his way, has fulfilled his duties with singular fidelity and success.

Since the writing of this report was commenced, some action has been taken which will largely increase the numbers of persons thrown on the protection of the Government. To-day, February 10th, the 47th Regiment New York Volunteers has been ordered to take military occupation of North Edisto Island, which is stated to have had formerly a population of 5000 or 6000, and a large number of plantations, a movement which involves great additional responsibility. Agents for the collection of cotton are to accompany it.

Herewith is communicated a copy of an order by General Sherman, dated February 6th, 1862, relative to the disposition of the plantations and of their occupants. It is an evidence of the deep interest which the Commanding General takes in this subject, and of his conviction that the exigency requires prompt and immediate action from the Government.

I leave for Washington, to add any oral explanations which may be desired, expecting to return at once, and, with the permission of the Department, to organize the laborers on some one plantation, and superintend them during the planting season, and upon its close, business engagements require that I should be relieved of this appointment.

I am, with great respect,

Your friend and servant,

EDWARD L. PIERCE.

EDUCATIONAL COMMISSION.

The Committee on Teachers and on Finance would call the attention of the friends of the Commission to the importance of additional subscription to its funds.

There are at Port Royal and other places, many thousands of colored persons, lately slaves, who are now under the protection of the U. S. Government. They are a well-disposed people, ready to work, and eager to learn. With a moderate amount of well-directed, systematic labor, they would very soon be able to raise crops more than sufficient for their own support. But they need aid and guidance in their first steps towards the condition of self-supporting, independent laborers.

It is the object of the Commission to give them this aid, by sending out, as agents, intelligent and benevolent persons, who shall instruct and care for them. These agents are called teachers, but their teaching will by no means be confined to intellectual instruction. It will include all the more important and fundamental lessons of civilization, — voluntary industry, self-reliance, frugality, forethought, honesty and truthfulness, cleanliness and order. With these will be combined intellectual, moral and religious instruction.

The plan is approved by the U. S. Government, and Mr. Edward L. Pierce, the Special Agent of the Treasury Department, is authorized to accept the services of the agents of this Commission, and to provide for them transportation, quarters and subsistence. Their salaries are paid by the Commission.

More than one hundred and fifty applications have been received by the Committee on Teachers, and thirty-five able and efficient persons have been selected. Twenty-nine of these sailed for Port Royal in the Atlantic, on the 3d instant. Three were already actively employed at that place, and the others are to follow by the next steamer. Some of these are volunteers, who gratuitously devote their time and labor to this cause. Others receive a monthly salary from the Commission.

The funds in the treasury, derived from voluntary and almost unsolicited contributions, are sufficient to support those now in service for two or three months. But the Commission is as yet only on the threshold of its undertaking. It is stated by Mr. Pierce that at least one hundred and fifty teachers could be advantageously employed in the vicinity of Port Royal alone.

Subscriptions may be sent to Mr. William Endicott, Jr., Treasurer, No. 33 Summer street, or to either of the Committee on Finance.

George B. Emerson,
Le Baron Russell,
Loring Lothrop,
Charles F. Barnard,
H. F. Stevenson,
Committee on Teachers.

Edward Atkinson,
Martin Brimmer,
William Endicott, Jr.,
James T. Fisher,
William I. Bowditch,
Committee on Finance.

Boston, March 14, 1862.

www.ingramcontent.com/pod-product-compliance
Lightning Source LLC
LaVergne TN
LVHW011123110826
845150LV00008B/2236

* 9 7 8 1 4 1 8 1 9 5 4 9 6 *